MOSCHINO

MOSCHINO

Edited by Samuele Mazza
Text by Mariuccia Casadio

Gingko
PRESS

On the cover
Couture!, 1997,
photograph by Ruven Afanador

On the back
'Whoever reads this is an ass!',
photograph by Ruven Afanador

Translation: Luciano Chianese

Art direction and design: Moschino

First published in Italy:
© 1997 by Leonardo Arte s.r.l., Milano, Elemond Editori Associati
All rights reserved

Published in the United States of America by Gingko Press Inc.
5768 Paradise Drive, Suite J - Corte Madera, CA 94925
Tel: (415) 924-9615 - Fax: (415) 924-9608 - email: gingko@linex.com

ISBN 3-927258-48-2

Printed in Italy

oschino has always been characterized by desecration, salvaging, irony and a taste for the topical, creating an intense stylistic collage of unprecedented combinations, a subtle mix of *double entendres*. From its very beginnings in 1983, the Moschino label has been synonymous with the utmost in freedom and creativity, always aiming to break free from the bonds of conventional fashion.

With Moschino, each person is allowed to help themselves or, as the British say, create their own 'self-made look'. In Franco Moschino's own words, 'I am like a chef in the sense that I follow classical recipes that time itself has invented.' This means choosing an item of clothing according to how you feel, in the same way that you are guided by appetite when deciding what to eat.

Followers of the Moschino image are undoubtedly sure of themselves, and use clothes as a form of self-expression. This intellectual attitude is often labelled 'radical chic'. Dress is a powerful form of communication for Moschino clients who challenge the conventional jacket-and-tie image.

As well as having seductive powers, clothes become objects to be enjoyed in their own right, reflecting the wearer's state of mind. And Moschino buyers have the added knowledge that they are doing something for the good of society, since Moschino is one of the few companies to be genuinely active in the field of charity work.

For many years now, the Franco Moschino Foundation has raised funds for a series of projects connected with HIV-positive children.

It was in 1988 that the Moschino label became a shareholding company owned by Moon Shadow S.p.A. The atmosphere within Moschino is bright and optimistic, but there is inevitably a degree of sadness on the frequent occasions when thoughts or conversation turn to the late master, who died so prematurely.

This volume is intended to be a tribute to one of the most important figures in modern society. I, for my part, have identified with his ironical and sacrilegious side, something I see as the 'ideal recipe' for the future of fashion, not only in Italy but throughout the world.

Samuele Mazza

The different lines
(Couture!, Cheap and
Chic, Jeans, Uomo)
for the 1997 publicity
campaign (the words,
like the models,
seen from behind).
Photograph by Ruven
Afanador.

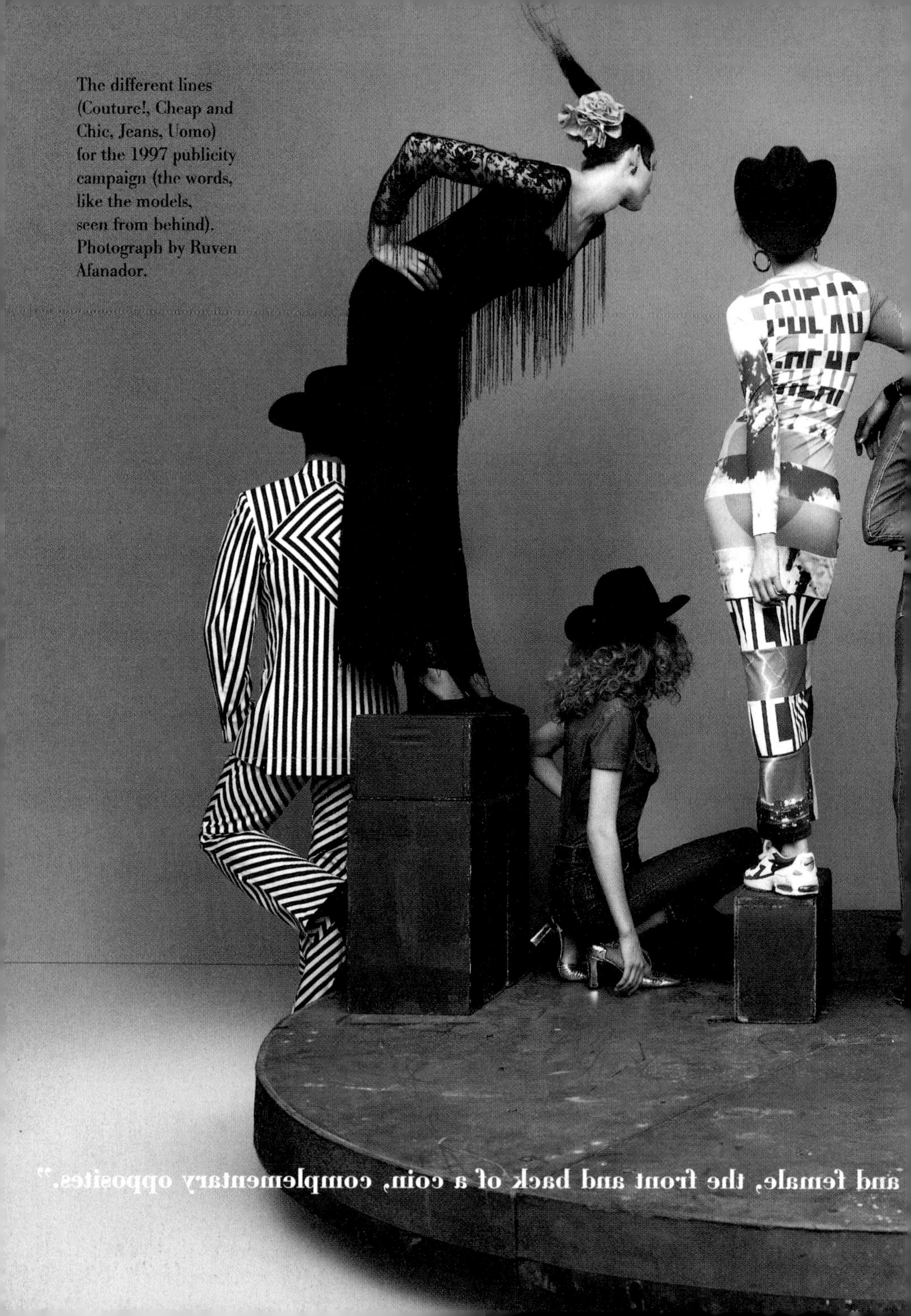

and female, the front and back of a coin, complementary opposites".

" The rational and the irrational, the positive and the negative, male

MOSCHINO

IN PIZZA WE TRUST

7991

The Recipe

On the one hand, to design, or rather, collect
the technical data and technological experience
of past centuries and ages;
on the other, to collect feelings, emotions and passions.
The rational and the irrational, the positive
and the negative, male and female,
the front and back
of a coin,
complementary opposites.
To mix the pieces and solve the puzzle.
To design, or rather, free oneself from technique
and emotion, to see the work
from the outside and to start playing,
experimenting first with one technique, one emotion,
then with others.

Jersey cotton T-shirt, on which is printed 'The Recipe', and a knitted viscose skirt with a ribbon embroidered with 'The Recipe'. Cheap and Chic, 1997, photograph by Ruven Afanador.

Page 8 Drawing by Franco Moschino for the shopping bag created for the Italian week at Bloomingdale's in New York, 1991.

Pages 9 and 11 'The Recipe', a text by Mauro Foroni on Moschino's philosophy.

, subtract, turn upside-down,
inside-out, test, reject.'
ix precision with irony, the patience
bers with childlike spontaneity,
echanics with the glow of mysticism.
ng as technique or sentiment
en't ends in themselves.
osites must coexist!
gination comes into play
the idea ends and love begins.
ithout speculation, without obligation.
nation is what
freely add
to a design.
It is said that artists are inspired
at night, on journeys, at the supermarket,
at the most unexpected moments.
Inspiration comes when
duty is done,
'so the idea also has a printed
heart!'
So far as the humour and irony
in Moschino's collections are concerned, they are
only two aspects of the thousand feelings
his projects are composed of.
Irony, provocation and humour
are safeguards against
design turning into a mission, or worse,
speculation.
Even though, unfortunately, they are often
the only elements recognized.
His tendency to play the leading role, also, is irony.

IN LOVE
WE
TRUST !

Names of the
Moschino team.

Rossella
Marco
Luigi
Angelo
Silvana Zafferri
Pellegrini
Caregaro
Claudia Firmani
Marini Luciano
Rubino Patrizia
Zegrini Joann Tan
Sergio Pandini
Castiglioni
RaffaellaBraghin
Paola Bertuzzi
Antonio Pippolini
Marzia Devoto Cinzia
Lida Castelli Romana
Massimo Storni
Somaruga
Zecchin
Annoni
Elisabetta
Umberto
Macchi
Laura
Mambretti
Fabrizio
Katia Tondi
Teresa
Radaelli

Jardini
Gobbetti
Martignoni
Moschino
Flavia
Annalisa
Gioconda Prandi
AnnePannier
Nigri Francesca
Rotondo Isabella
Remo Macco
Francesca
Valentina Biondi
RobertoBuratti
ElisaPalomino
PaoloPascolo
Paolo Pascolo
Mottola
Rocchi
Gianpiero
Paola
Cristina
Vismara
Braghin
Patrizia
Arienti
Fabio
Morin
antiello
Fossati
Nadia
Uccellat

Luca Di
Marco Nereo Friso
Cristina Bernardi Claudia
Rossi Antonello Annunziata
Valentina   Israel Sarah
Kulyan   Rossella
Jardini   Marco
Gobbetti   Luigi
Martignoni   Angelo
Moschino   Silvana
Zafferri   Flavia
Pellegrini   Annalisa
Caregaro   Gioconda
Prandi   Claudia
Firmani   Anne
Marini   Pannier
Luciano   Nigri
Francesca   Rubino
Patrizia   Rotondo
Isabella   Zegrini
Joann Tan   Remo
Macco   Sergio
Pandini   Francesca
Castiglioni   Valentina
Biondi   Raffaella
Braghin   Roberto
Buratti   Paola
Bertuzzi   Elisa
Palomino Antonio Pippolini
Paolo Pascolo Marzia
Devoto Cinzia

Mottola
Lida Castelli
Romana   Rocchi
Massimo   Storni
Giampiero   Sommarru
Barbara   Veggetti
Paola   Zecchin
Laura   Cordovani
Cristina   Annoni
Stefania
Vismara
Elisabetta
Vidali Donata
Braghin Mario
Crastolla
Umberto
Passannante
Marcello
Moretti
Massimo
Dottore
Vincenzo   Bonanno
Luciano   Serra
Maria   Belloni
Daniela   Laboranti
Gerry   Velasquez
Ymeghen   Ghirmay
Dolores   Bonezzi
Veronica Moise Oscar
Pacchioni Alessandra
Sechi Leo Febrizio

F
Yuki
Giovanna
Shapiro A
Dorota
ka Armand
Luca
Annelisa
Mattia
Pietro
Paolo Frara
Fabio
Cagnetta
Massimo
Scognamig
lio Petra
Scholer
Isabella
Venzo
Maria
Poletto
Patrizia
Marcello
Laura
Fabio
Marta
Fabrizio
o Katia
Andrea F
Cappelli
Daniel

o o
illiam
hhoner
wandos
Chitolina
acco
accheria
resp i
Messaggi

Macchi
rienti
Goluya
Mambretti
Quarantiell
o n d i
Teresa
daelli
tor

A n n a
o Charo
Luca Di
N e r e o
Cristina
Claudia
Antonello
a Valentina
S a r a h
Rossella
M a r c o
L u i g i
i Angelo
Silvana
Flavia Pellegrini
Caregaro Gioconda
Claudia Firmani
M a r i n i
N i g r i
R u b i n o
Rotondo
Z e g r i n i
R e m o
S e r g i o
Francesca
Valentina
Raffaella
Roberto
P a o l a
E l i s a
Antonio

Borraccin
P e r a l t a
M a r c o
F r i s o
Bernardi
R o s s i
Annunziat
I s r a e l
K u l y a n
J a r d i n i
Gobbetti
Martignon
Moschino
Zafferri
Annalisa
Prandi
Anne Pannier
Luciano
Francesca
Patrizia
Isabella
Joann Tan
M a c c o
Pandini
Castiglioni
B i o n d i
Braghin
Buratti
Bertuzzi
Palomino
Pippolini

P a o l o
Pascolo
M a r z i a
D e v o t o
C i n z i a
Mottola
L i d a
Castelli
R o m a n a
R o c c h i
Massimo
S t o r n i
Gianpiero
Sommaruga
B a r b a r a
Veggetti
P a o l a
Zecchin
L a u r a
Cordovani
Cristina
Annoni
Stefania
Vismara
Elisabetta
Vidali
Donata
Braghin
Umberto
Passannante
Patrizia

M a c c h i
Arienti
Goluya Fabio
Marta Morin
Quarantiello
Tondi Andrea
Teresa Cappelli
Radaelli Daniele
Anna Borraccino
Peralta Luca Di
Nereo Friso
BernardiClaudia
Antonello Annun
Valentina Israel
K u l y a n Marcello
Massimo Dottore
Bonanno LucianoS
M a r i a Belloni
Laboranti Gerry
Ghirmay Ymeghen
B o n e z z i Veronica
Pacchioni Alessandra
Sechi Leo
Y u k i e
Giovanna
William
A n n a
D o r o t a
a Armando
L u c a
Annelisa

Marcello
L a u r a
Mambretti
Fabrizio
K a t i a
Fossati
N a d i a
Poletto
C h a r o
M a r c o
Cristina
R o s s i
z i a t a
S h a r a
Moretti
Vincenzo
e r r a
Daniela
Velasquez
Dolores
Oscar
Alessandra
Fabrizio
Y o k o o
Villani
Shapiro
Wemhoner
Lewandosk
Chitolina
Z a c c o
Zaccheria

Mattia
Crespi Pietro
Messaggi Paolo Frara
Fabio Cagnetta Massimo
Scognamig   lio Petra
Scholer   Isabella
V e n z o   M a r i a
P o l e t t o   Rossella
J a r d i n i   M a r c o
Gobbetti   L u i g i
Martignon i   A n g e l o
Moschino   Silvana
Z a f f e r r i   F l a v i a
Pellegrini   Annalisa
Caregaro   Gioconda
P r a n d i   Claudia
Firmani   A n n e
Pannier   M a r i n i
Luciano   N i g r i
Francesca   R u b i n o
Patrizia   Rotondo
Isabella   Z e g r i n i
Joann Tan   R e m o
M a c c o   S e r g i o
Pandini   Francesca
Castiglioni   Valentina
B i o n d i   Raffaella
Braghin   Roberto
Buratti Paola Bertuzzi Elisa
Palomino Antonio
P i p p o l i n i

Lace-effect wool
top. Couture!,
1997–98,
photograph by
Ruven Afanador.

*trompe l'œil* fabric simulates a brick wall, part of a building that shuns any disguise or embellishment that one might expect – no paint, touching up or other decoration; in this perfect metaphor of Moschino style we find an unmistakable link with fashion. Moschino was the first to transform the mania for designer labels into a creative and conscious extension of personality. He encouraged the invention of an aesthetic identity that is both sensitive and sexual, choosing its wardrobe without constraint, and defining its own lifestyle. '*De gustibus non est disputandum*', or 'If you can't be elegant, at least be extravagant', is just one of the many slogans, which come in the form of set phrases, proverbs and rhyming couplets, adopted by Moschino and his team that reflect the highly developed nature of their theoretical concepts, their sense of humour and the strength of their convictions. From an island characterized by direct provocation, screaming symbols and skies teeming with angels, archangels, cherubim and other religious images, the Moschino message is always explicit. It is up front and in your face, like a row of gilded buttons, and is forever the theme of shirts, T-shirts, pleats, seams and ruffles.

From the outset in the mid-eighties, Moschino and his carefully chosen group of 'accomplices' were more akin to an avant-garde art movement or a modern adventure story than to a routine and methodical fashion enterprise. Moschino had a completely unique vision of the industry, tinged with a good deal of philosophy. With narrative flair, words accompanied fashion images in a manifestation of true poetic passion. Moschino loved the sumptuous red velvet of stage curtains and the theatrical nature of communication. He transformed single letters and graphics into black-and-white conceptual icons, creating visual puns. It was no coincidence that Fornasetti's influence was an obsession within the workshop and often guided the designer's choice of form. Moschino's repertoire of influences ranges from Marcel Duchamp's playful and transgressive Dada chessboard to the famous star-shaped hair tonsure and to the artist dressing up as Rrose Sélavy, all deftly hybridized with more Mannerist touches. Amid an abundance of stylized neo-Baroque curls, vulgar and over-the-top historical references and wonderfully fake and anachronistic gilding

are found throughout the workshop, boutiques, paintings and advertising campaigns. All the cultural, artistic or creative elements introduced into Moschino imagery over the years still play a fundamental and recurrent role today as some of the many ingredients that constitute Moschino's unique recipe for style and define its rapport with the fashion industry. Through art, performances and a passion for the provocative and unconventional, ever present in its designs, as well as through a unique conception of exhibiting space and an understanding of gesture and pose, Moschino still holds a prominent intellectual position in fashion. Consequently it is not difficult to recognize the designer's critical and speculative talents, embodied in his choice of influences. He incorporated into his work elements of those he admired and deemed to be the makers of the twentieth-century avant-garde. He has drawn on a range of inspirations; from uniforms to Chanel and Burberry's and from the costumes of classical theatre to seventeenth-century lace and crochetwork. Not to mention Harlequin masks; the kaleidoscopic allure of patchwork; the immortal charisma of denim; huge earrings; JR Ewing-style hats; ice-cold gazes hiding behind black Persol sunglasses; an ironic passion for Hermès checks; and Yves Saint Laurent-style safari jackets. Moschino style is governed by freedom of interpretation. Escaping not only from the ghetto of momentary trend, but also from the trap of seasons and collections, Moschino destroys the myth that fashion must be original and serialized.

In his autobiography, Moschino wrote with his scathingly paradoxical pen and free, ironic use of words: 'Once upon a time I was in a house near a big city and I wanted to paint the clothes of the Madonnas and meet the Angels. Everyone always told me that you couldn't and shouldn't. So, after thinking about it a great deal, I walked towards where I thought the Angels and the Madonnas were. I walked and walked, and after a long time I found myself with a golden brush, painting the stars on the sky blue cape of a Lady standing on a white cloud. There were Angels all around joking with me. Someone asked me to paint other clothes, and wanted to introduce me to other

Lace dress with fringes. Couture!, 1997, photograph by Helmut Newton for Italian *Vogue*.

Angels. I don't want to paint other clothes, I don't know who they're for, I don't want to meet other Angels, because they wouldn't joke with me. Leave me here on my white cloud.'

Just like a Zen meditation, a half moon, a pizza, a question mark or a heart, the above tale turns back on itself and leads off in unexpected and different directions. Riding on his cloud, Moschino escapes the greyness of banality, boredom and predictability. Progressing from vanity to social and humanist activism – from the inward smile of the audience to the 'Smile!' project – the story unfolds to communicate a universal message of commitment. At first collaborating with Anlaids, in 1993 Moschino set out to provide both holiday houses and permanent homes for a heartrending and very real number of HIV-positive children. Following these early initiatives, the Franco Moschino Foundation was founded as an autonomous charity in 1995. From Italy to Romania, it organizes holidays for sick children, setting up and running a number of projects aimed at providing cures and support for these youngsters, who have been institutionalized in hospitals and orphanages. The Franco Moschino Foundation has lent extra voice to that rich, philosophical and human chorus with which Moschino challenges the predictability of the fashion business. With the ironic Olive Oil, huge crowns and leashed geese, we can be sure that Moschino will not only continue but increase the commitments it has already made through to the next millennium. From the year 2000 and forever, Moschino can rely on the tireless and loyal support of his appointed heirs, of those who today ride on that same white cloud and bear witness to an apparently untarnishable integrity. Creative geniuses, friends and collaborators continue to realize stylistic ideas, initiatives and projects while maintaining a commitment to the concerns of today's society. The memory of Franco and his enthusiasm is forever present to comfort them, like the phone calls of someone reporting home from abroad.

Silk cady jacket, hand printed to create a soft hound's-tooth check effect. Couture!, 1997, photograph by Paolo Roversi for *Catalogo Neiman Marcus*.

The Leaning Tower of Pisa.

Tweed dress with lace ruche. Couture!,
1996–97, photograph by Lillian
Bassman for *Catalogo Neiman Marcus*.

Wool satin jacket
with a flame-
effect print.
Couture!,
1997–98,
photograph by
Ruven Afanador.

Lace mantilla
and velvet wings.
Couture!,
1995–96,
photograph by
Giampaolo
Barbieri.

I t's all so simple' accompanies Moschino shows like a signature, an unmistakable phrase that aptly describes an attitude to fashion that has characterized Moschino from the start and will lead it harmoniously towards the future. An empire of ideas, Moschino philosophy also feeds a financial empire and testifies to a success that stems from far-sighted ideas and a belief in the personality of the fashion consumer.

It is not easy to summarize a style based on the total freedom to combine different items of clothing. No fashion show before Moschino contained such high doses of humour and energy. Once the barriers that separated jeans and couture were broken down, along with those that divided menswear from womenswear and underwear from tailored jackets, Moschino shows were used to communicate concepts rather than merely to present his products in an expensive and excessively institutional way. This led during the late eighties to the use of short videos, which worked as catalogues, displaying a selection of garments from the collection that was being launched. Viewings were by appointment, which gave clients added contact with the fabrics, cuts and colours. More importantly, these private viewings enabled clients to talk to the designer directly as well as giving him brief respite from the frenzied crowd of fashion specialists.

The nineties have witnessed a slow rekindling of an early Moschino hallmark – the ability to turn a fashion show into a performance, always different, surprising and deeply ironic. This tendency has been continued through the years thanks to the talents of the Moschino team, who wish to guarantee the vitality and success of a truly modern style.

Although certain figures or aesthetic trends often return in cycles, talented designers never re-use them in exactly the same way. Nothing is really taken seriously, from Andalusian flair to the aplomb of classic Western elegance. In both informal and flawless reconstructions of beauty, the ability to play on an error of syntax, on the unfinished, is a feature of Moschino that stands out, brimming with energy and genius. The use of prints that make a jacket and trousers seem like two pages that have been stuck together gives the impression that Moschino, by prising open these pages, is revealing his most secret fashion recipes to the public. With his hearts, ruches, leather and denim jackets, and in both new and classic styles, the memory of Moschino is omnipresent during the planning of fashion shows, exhibitions, books and brochures.

'To be, or not to be, that's fashion!', 'Love has no colours' and 'You can't judge a girl by her clothes' are just some of the slogans that continue to transform an item of clothing into a vehicle of communication and a tangible projection of the wearer's personality.

The key to Moschino's success undoubtedly lies in his ability to identify with ideologies and styles without losing sight of his own ideals, often creating direct and strong links with a world governed by quite different and disparate needs. Moschino invents a mosaic of cake-shaped bags, of perfumes as inviting as soft drinks and of ironic interpretations of the styling concepts that dictate fashion, while ignoring a conventional sense of time, passing trends and binding iconographic rules. Little by little, through live animals, condoms, 'for sale' signs and the graphics of mail-order catalogues, a spirit of our time emerges. Moschino highlights the cruelties and paradoxes of contemporary culture, the endlessly regenerated power of the ready-made and the din of forms and banality by which we are controlled and surrounded. As if in a cathartic ritual, Moschino fashion shows are like a mirror, forcing us to acknowledge the reflection of the world around us, a world we cannot escape. And yet the awareness of our limitations and stupidity does not offend us, but instead gives us an unexpected feeling of strength and self.

Pages 26–27 Silk satin suit printed with a collage designed by Franco Moschino. Couture!, 1995–96, photograph by Giampaolo Barbieri.

Page 28 Crêpe sheath dress embroidered with 'It's all so simple'. Couture!, 1996, photograph by Stefano Pandini.

Stretch viscose jersey T-shirt printed with 'Now is all there is' and crêpe skirt printed with the famous sunglasses. Couture!, 1997, illustration by François Berthoud for German *Vogue*, March 1997.

Cotton poplin
shirt. Couture!,
1996, photograph
by Paolo Roversi
for Italian *Vogue*.

Cotton poplin shirt,
crêpe stitched top
and braided calf
belt. Couture!,
1997, photograph
by Ruven Afanador.

モスキノ

は寿司が好きです

MOSCHINO LIKES SUSHI

Page 34 Fake
hair bustier and
skirt consisting
of a collage of
plastic-coated
cards, with a
photographic
print of a geisha
girl's face, fixed to
a crêpe base with
a 'price tagger'.
Couture!, 1997,
photograph by
Ruven Afanador.

Stretch cotton
poplin kimono.
Couture!, 1997,
photograph by
Patrick Shaw for
British *Marie
Claire*.

Pages 38–39
Stretch wool
dress with a zip
fastener that
follows the line
of the body.
Couture!,
1996–97,
photograph by
Robin Derrick
for British *Vogue*,
Condé Nast PL.

Right Inflatable
PVC suit.
Couture!,
1996–97,
photograph
by Platon.

Crêpe sheath
dress with
inflatable PVC
stole. Couture!,
1996–97,
photograph
by Platon.

Three dresses
covered in
plastic-coated
cards, with a
photographic
print of the Taj
Mahal. Couture,
1997, photograph
by Fleto Biasion

Lurex silk
jacquard dress.
'Couture'. 1997.
photograph by
Torkil Gudnason
for *Amica*

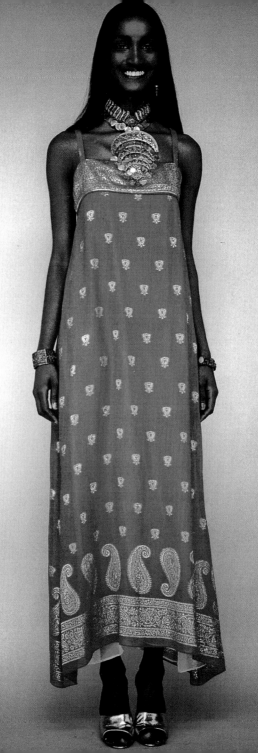

Shirley Manson
wearing a 'Ladybird'
dress in crêpe and
silk satin. Couture!.
1995-96.
photograph by
Gilles Bensimon
for American *Elle*.

'Bouquet' dress
with silk flowers
and a bow made
from florist's
paper. Couture!.
1997. photograph
by Piero Biasion.

Fake leather and
nylon jacket.
Jeans Uomo,
1997, photograph
by Ruven
Afanador.

Viscose dévoré
dress with silk
flowers and
butterflies attached.
Couture!, 1997,
photograph by
Judson Baker
for *Amica*.

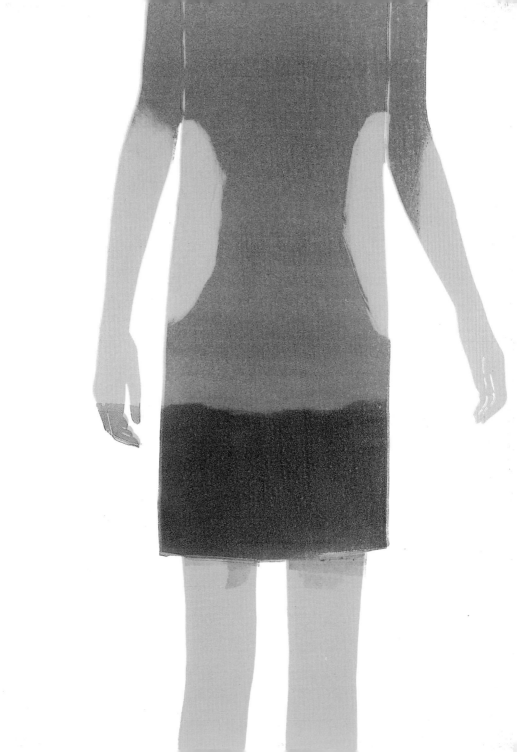

Page 48 Tie-
dyed handmade
silk chiffon dress.
Couture!, 1997,
photograph by
Christophe Rihet
for German
Amica.

Page 49 Hand-
painted woollen
fabric sheath
dress. Couture!,
1997, illustration
by François
Berthoud for
German *Vogue*,
March 1997.

Lined wool coat
with fake mink
collar. Couture!,
1996–97,
photograph by
Marc de Groot
for Dutch *Elle*.

Ecological
woollen fabric
dress with a
gorilla printed
in vegetable
dyes. Couture!,
1994–95,
photograph by
Mike Reinhardt
for American *Elle*.

Finale of the
'X Anni di Kaos!'
fashion show,
October 1993.

Symbol of
the Franco
Moschino
Foundation.

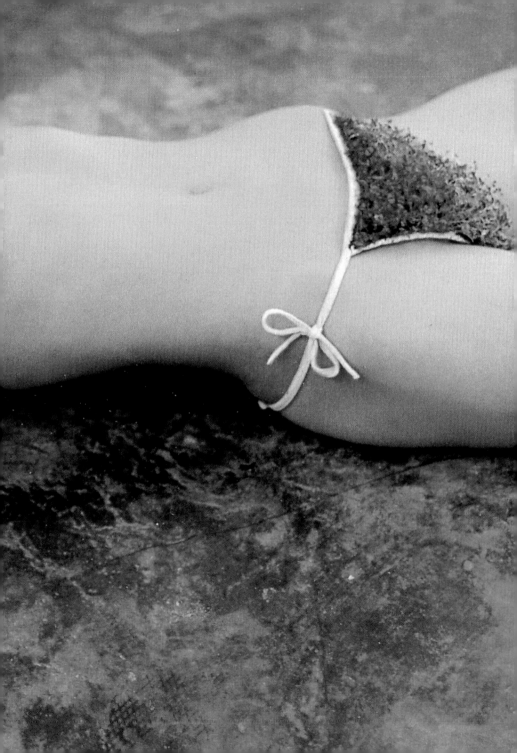

Page 54 Satin backed cady dress with photosensitive flowers that change colour with exposure to light. Cheap and Chic, 1997, photograph by Francesca Lotti for Spanish *Vogue*.

Page 55 Ecological jacket in wool gauze with a cotton tulle border. Cheap and Chic, 1995–96, photograph by Platon.

Pages 56–57 'Organic' bikini created by sowing and watering the material. Photograph by Tiziano Magni for *Sports Illustrated*.

Left Military-style overcoat in woollen covert coating and gold sequin dress. Cheap and Chic, 1996–97, photograph by Robert Erdmann for British *Vogue*, Condé Nast PL.

Right Cotton and viscose flying suit. Cheap and Chic, 1997, photograph by Inez van Lamsweerde-Vinoodh Matadino for *The Face*.

Wool satin skirt
printed with a
cartoon silhouette.
Cheap and Chic,
1995–96,
photograph by
Gerald Klepka
for *Bolero*.

Velvet jacket
printed with
graphic artwork.
Cheap and Chic,
1996–97,
photograph
by Platon.

Lycra bra and pants worn over stretch satin trousers and jersey top. Cheap and Chic, 1997, photograph by Hiro Masa for *L'Officiel Paris*, April 1997.

Body Art (striped top painted on skin) and crêpe sailors' trousers. Cheap and Chic, 1996, photograph by Platon.

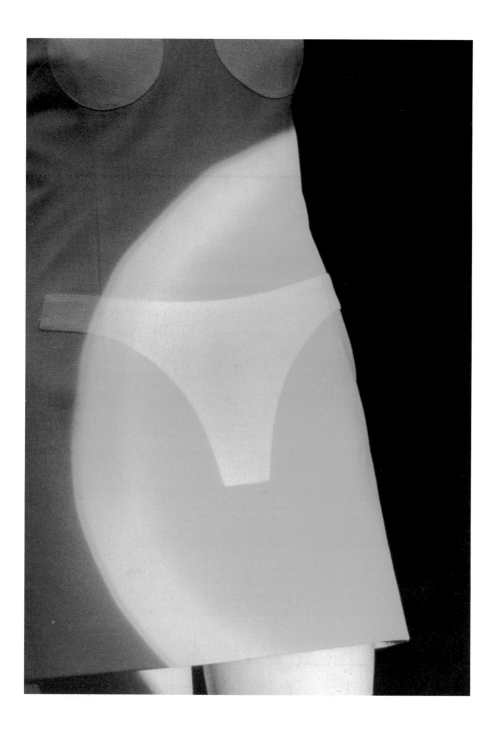

YOU CAN'T JUDGE A GIRL BY HER CLOTHES

Page 66 Cady dress with a bikini in photosensitive material. Cheap and Chic, 1997, photograph by Piero Biasion.

Page 67 Velvet top and tulle skirt. Cheap and Chic, 1995–96, photograph by Craig McDean for *W*.

Page 69 Organzine parka dress with hood. Cheap and Chic, 1997–98, photograph by Ruven Afanador.

Right Lycra dress with a printed and inlaid graffiti effect. Cheap and Chic, 1997, photograph by Torkil Gudnadson for German *Vogue*, April 1997.

To be, or not to be, that's fashion !

Page 73 Cotton
gabardine suit with
a photographic
print of geese.
Cheap and Chic
Uomo, 1996–97,
photograph by
Piero Biasion.

Right Black wool
gabardine suit.
Cheap and Chic
Uomo, 1997–98,
photograph by
Ruven Afanador.

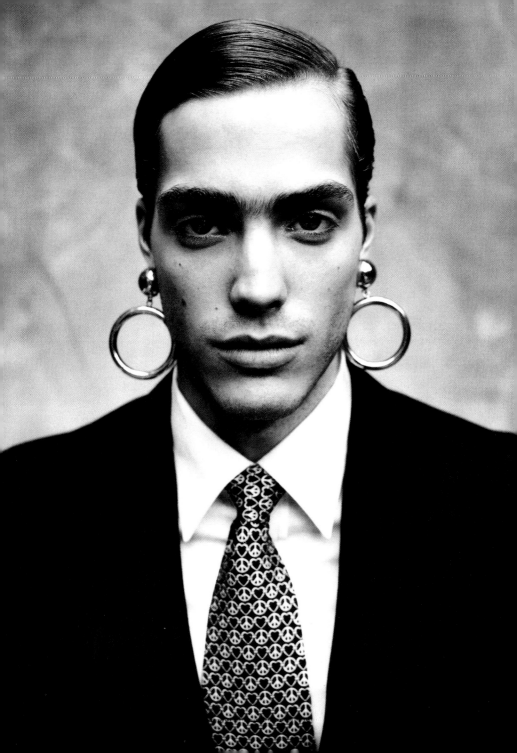

Cotton gabardine trousers with a 'supermarket' print. Jeans Uomo, 1996, photograph by Max Dereta for British *Esquire*.

Cotton satin jacket with a sunset and palm tree print. Cheap and Chic Uomo, 1996, photograph by Dah Len for *Mondo Uomo*.

Image used to
promote the
Underwear
collection.
Photograph by
Stefano Pandini.

Men's lycra
swimwear. Mare
Uomo, 1996,
photograph by
Gianni Gravina
for *Mondo Uomo*.

I am *still* *what* I am!

Invitation to the Couture! 1995–96 fashion show.

Cotton poplin optical suit. Cheap and Chic Uomo, 1997, photograph by Ruven Afanador.

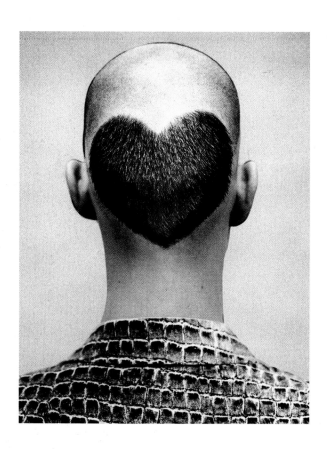

Cotton velvet
jacket with a
crocodile print.
Cheap and Chic
Uomo, 1996–97,
photograph by
Platon.

Press campaign
for the Occhiali
(Glasses) 1997
collection. Tartan-
effect tulle T-shirt
printed with 'The
Recipe'. Cheap

and Chic, 1997,
photograph by
Ruven Afanador.

Denim and stretch chambray all-in-one. Jeans, 1997, photograph by Ruven Afanador.

REAMS
CAN
COME
TRUE

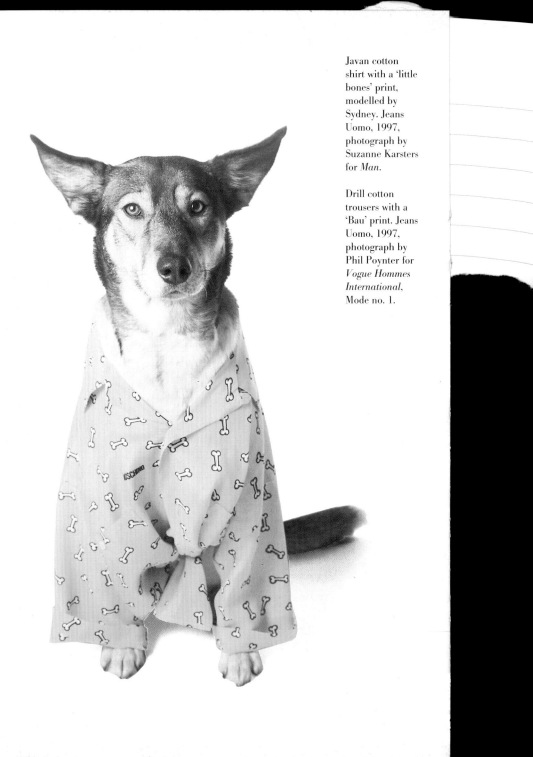

Javan cotton shirt with a 'little bones' print, modelled by Sydney. Jeans Uomo, 1997, photograph by Suzanne Karsters for *Man*.

Drill cotton trousers with a 'Bau' print. Jeans Uomo, 1997, photograph by Phil Poynter for *Vogue Hommes International*, Mode no. 1.

Photograph donated to the
'Moda e Gioielli, Uniti nella
Lotta all'Aids' (Fashion and
Jewelry, United in the Battle
against Aids) exhibition,
organized by Bulgari in
support of the Aids Solidarity
Association. 1997, photograph
by Ruven Afanador.

The Moschino
earring.

Gold laminated
fake leather
jacket. Jeans,
1997–98,
photograph by
Ruven Afanador.

L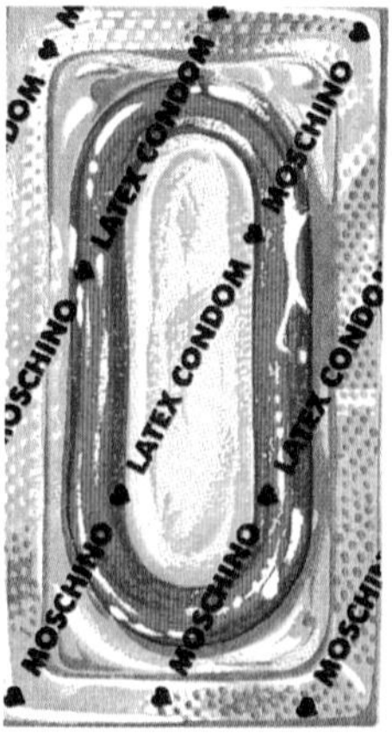VE

Heart-shaped
bag. 1996–97,
photograph by
Michelangelo
di Battista.

'Coffeeproof' sofa
in white vinyl with
embroidery and
inlay. Madison
Avenue boutique,
New York.

'Chocolate' bag.
1996, photograph
by Giampaolo
Barbieri.

Pages 96–97
Union Jack suede
shoes. 1993–94,
photograph by
Stefano Pandini.

Above and right
Advertisement
for Cheap and
Chic perfume.
December 1996,
photographs by
Stefano Pandini.

Far right Press
campaign for
Cheap and Chic
perfume. 1996,
photograph by
Platon.

10. " SENZA TITOLO "

" UNTITLED "

In line with Moschino's policy of introducing humour to culture, a white T-shirt has replaced the more traditional artist's canvas and pokes fun at the stiff ideas of the establishment. As well as being a figurative monochrome, the T-shirt is also a minimalist image, bearing traces of Pop art, and forms part of a series of initiatives grouped under the slogan 'Take Art and Set It Apart'. The white T-shirt therefore acts as an introduction to that paradoxically serious yet humorous link between Moschino's ideas and the most outrageous events in contemporary art.

In a genre all to himself, Moschino, in his search for total freedom of expression, has always been determined to avoid any form of categorization or definition. Moschino style flits between stereotypes in fashion and in art; it breaks the rules of linguistic syntax and shuns traditional interpretation, reinventing words and images by imbuing them with totally new and individual meanings. A stranger to the world of convention, predictability and Western rituals and ideals, Moschino is a master of restyling as well as an inventor and reinventor of new cultural, chromatic and formal combinations. While adverse to intellectualisms, Moschino remains one of the most intellectual figures on the fashion scene from the Second World War through to the third millennium.

Always striving to go against the grain, the Moschino team has succeeded in transcending boundaries without ever overdoing it or losing a sense of spontaneity. Fuelled by a conception of personality as being a deceptive yet playful *alter ego*, the Moschino label continues to influence contemporary culture and to undermine its predictability. It is only in this context that we have allowed art to enter the realms of fashion and witnessed a degree of symbiosis between the art of fashion and the fashion for art. The languages of two of today's most widespread forms of communication have now harmoniously joined to form a complete circle, inextricably linked by an almost inalienable series of messages, which may be implicit or explicit, but are all 'committed',

Untitled by Franco Moschino, 1988. Created for the 'To Be, or Not to Be, That's Fashion!' launch exhibition of the Uomo 1988–89 collection.

Some of the works of art sold at the 'Art is Love' auction organized in aid of Hale House, Harlem, to celebrate the opening of the New York boutique in October 1996. *Left-hand page, clockwise from the top* Donald Baechler, *Untitled*, George Condo, *Antipodal Shopper*, Ronnie Cutrone, *Raggedy Andy*.

From the top Kenny Scharf, *Moskenny Scharfino Fashionella*, John Baldassari, *Nine Personality Types*.

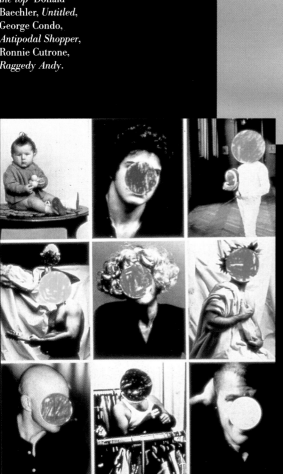

Khadija

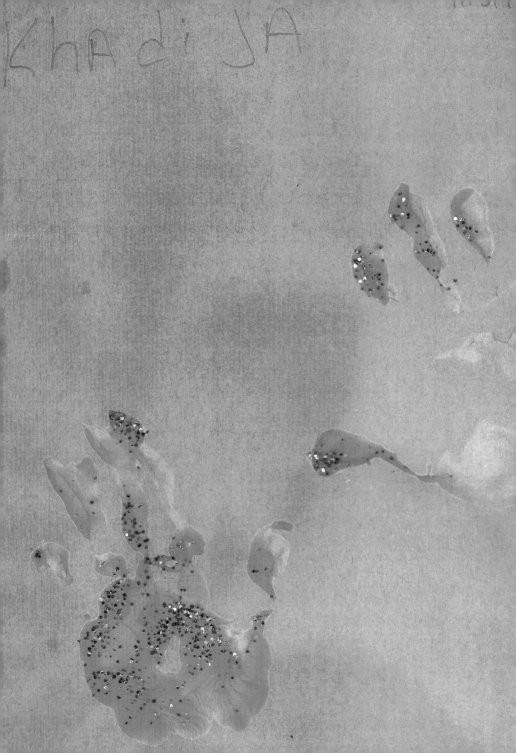

either socially, humanistically or existentially. This is confirmed by ideas and projects that all bear the Moschino hallmark, an identity that is constantly reinforced by a continuum of symbols, recollections and creative happenings.

Among these was 'Art is Love' (New York, October 1996), a charity event in aid of the famous Hale House in Harlem, a home for the children of alcoholics, drug-addicts and AIDS-sufferers. Eighteen top international artists including Arman, Julian Schnabel, George Condo, Donald Baechler and John Baldessari were invited to produce works inspired by the interpretation of Moschino imagery. An auction, 'One Night Event', was then held and the proceeds went to charity. Other precious funds were raised at a party held on the same night to inaugurate Moschino's new boutique on Madison Avenue. The party must certainly go on. On 30 October, Olive Oil, the 'ideal woman' from the Cheap and Chic line, made an appearance at the CFDA Pavilion at New York's Bryant Park with a host of ideas for Spring/Summer 1997. At the same time the Moschino staff were reaping other essential, if less spectacular, fruits from a curious and absent-mindedly co-operative crowd of society party-goers.

For some time now, a large heart has been one of the principal icons in Moschino imagery. Versatile in meaning, the heart can represent ecology, peace and criticism of the fashion industry, and it became the main symbol of the 'New Persona, New Universe' project, inaugurated at the Florence Biennale in September 1996. For the event, Moschino installed a heart-shaped maze accompanied by a laconic quotation from Pascal, 'The heart has its reasons that know no reason.' Traced in generous curves, the heart represents a journey punctuated with pauses, observations and reflections – a large-scale invitation to listen and dwell on the causes of one's feelings; it symbolizes an attempt at engaging in a dialogue with the natural dimension. Furthermore, the heart encourages the acceptance of one's own uniqueness, one's living in harmony with the cycles of the earth, the skies and the elements. Visitors made their way

Drawing by Khadi Ja, one of the children staying at Hale House, Harlem.

105

Sketches and drawings for the installation project for the 'New Persona, New Universe' exhibition at the Florence Biennale. Stazione Leopolda, 1996.

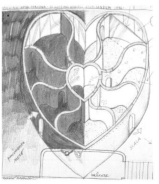

Pages 108–9 The heart-shaped maze installation for the 'New Persona, New Universe' exhibition at the Florence Biennale. Stazione Leopolda, 1996. Photographs by Attilio Maranzano.

through the network of soft, inflatable arteries that were kept open and pulsating by ventilators. In this way, the labyrinthine structure allowed spectators to embark on a pleasurable journey beyond space and time, without the fear of losing their way and consequently needing to find an exit. As in Moschino's best-loved fairy tales, the heart provided a happy ending in as much as it was a metaphor for a world in which, in the wake of sinister spells and magical intervention, everyone can live happily ever after.

The concept behind the heart installation in Florence, of providing pleasure, relief and unity, was also the driving force behind the 'Moschino for Sarajevo 2000' project. This exhibition opened on 12 June 1997 and was held at the Querini Stampalia Foundation as part of the Venice Biennale. Another tale with a happy ending, this idea was born in July 1992, just three months into Sarajevo's siege.

Ten contemporary European art museums and galleries have been invited to donate works to reestablish the modern art museum in Sarajevo, due to be rebuilt by the year 2000 – a dream come true. The exhibition featured works by Alighiero Boetti, Nan Goldin, Ilya Kabakov, Joseph Kosuth, Julian Opie, Mimmo Paladino, Remo Salvadori, Cindy Sherman and Rosemarie Trockel. The success of the exhibition bears witness to Moschino's image and the fame of its publicity campaigns. With the Moschino label always linked to messages of protest, provocation and the birth of new social values, the exhibition is another episode in the continuing series of events that, season after season, make Moschino one of the most integral and respected cultural phenomena of our times. The list of happy endings grows ever longer as the association between history, current affairs and Moschino's ideology grows ever stronger, forming a mosaic that is continuously subject to unexpected reinvention.

Some of the
memorable faces
used to launch
Moschino
publicity
campaigns.

Franco Moschino
in disguise
launches the
1989 Couture!
collection.
Photograph by
Stefano Pandini.

Window display
at the Los
Angeles boutique
on Rodeo Drive.

The 'Label
Queen' dress
created from
shopping bags
and labels for a
window display

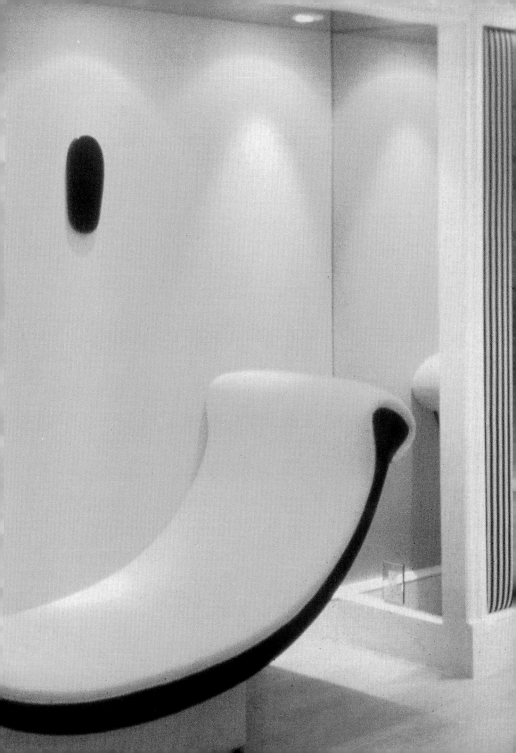

Moschino Boutiques

Italy
Via Sant'Andrea 12, Milan
Via Durini 14, Milan
Via Borgognona 32, Rome
Via Belsiana 57, Rome

United States
803 Madison Avenue, New York
362 North Rodeo Drive, Los Angeles

Japan
4-23-11 Minami Aoyama, Tokyo
Ritz Carlton Hotel, Herbis Plaza, Osaka
Kobe-Daimaru Block 30, Kobe

Thailand
153 Peninsula Plaza, Bangkok

Indonesia
Plaza Senayan, Jakarta

Malaysia
50 Jalan Sultan Ismail, Kuala Lumpur

Singapore
Hilton Hotel, 581 Orchard Road, Singapore

Hong Kong
Swire House, Shop 11A, Hong Kong
The Regent Hotel, Hong Kong
Ocean Terminal, Hong Kong

Taiwan
Da-an Road, Taipei
69 Wu Fu Three Road, Kaoshiung

Guam
Tumon Sands Plaza, Tumond

Pages 116–17 The stairwell of
The 'Smile!' sofa   the New York
in cotton satin   boutique; the
made for the New   wrought-iron and
York boutique.   brass banisters
                    are shaped as
                    question marks.

Drawing by
Franco Moschino
for a hat in the
shape of a
wedding cake.

Chronology

1950

Franco Moschino is born at Abbiategrasso in the province of Milan.

1967–69

Moschino attends the Accademia di Belle Arti di Brera in Milan. After finishing his studies and a number of different jobs, he works as an illustrator on various magazines: *Gap, Linea Italiana, Harper's Bazaar*.

1972–77

Moschino begins to work as an illustrator with Gianni Versace.

1978–83

For eleven seasons he designs Cadette's collections, which, as he himself admits, 'already present various "anomalies" towards the established rules of fashion'. During that time, he also acts as an adviser for Dejac (1977–81), Matti (1980–87), Lesy (1982–84), Maska (1983–84), Helyett (1983–85), Lorenzini (1984–87), Alberto Aspesi (1984–88), Enrico Mandelli (1985–88), Blumarine (1985–87), Armonia (1987) and Gianna Cassoli (1988–89).

1983

On 7 October the first Moschino womenswear collection (Summer 1984) is shown at the Fiera di Milano, produced by Ditta Aeffe. Moschino, inventor of a new and provocative way of presenting fashion, is branded by the press as 'transgressive', an 'Enfant terrible', a 'Bad Boy'.
In May Moschino S.n.c. becomes Moon Shadow S.r.l., a limited company.

1985

Moschino takes part in the 'Italia: The Genius of Fashion' exhibition, organized by the Fashion Institute of Technology at the Shirley Goodman Resource Center in New York.

1986

The first menswear collection (Summer 1986) is presented at the Sala delle Cariatidi at the Palazzo Reale in Milan, with an exhibition of garments for the male wardrobe displayed as fake works of contemporary art. The following collection (1986–87) is presented at the Villa Reale in Milan, which was specially transformed into a Neapolitan market for the event.

1987

Franco Moschino takes part in the television programme *Una Notte di moda* (A Night of Fashion), singing 'Reginella'; it is broadcast live on Italian national television.

An enormous party with a fairground theme, complete with sideshows, dance competitions, target shooting and custard-pie throwing, launches the first Moschino perfume. At the entrance a fake exhibition 'Storia del Profumo nei Secoli' (The History of Perfume over the Centuries) is mounted.

1988

The first womenswear Cheap and Chic collection is launched (1988–89).

The first fake furs appear in the 'Fur for Fun' collection.

The entire Missoni team dress up as Father Christmas to produce a seasonal video, shown in several Italian cinemas, in which they sing 'We wish you a Merry Christmas'.

The Autumn/Winter 1988–89 collections are presented at 'The Grand Parade', a large circus-fashion show at the Rolling Stone, a night club in Milan. The Couture!, men's and women's Cheap and Chic, Jeans and Bambino collections are all shown amid a crowd of majorettes, acrobats, a band, jesters, clowns and other figures from the circus.

'Moschino a Medianoche' (Moschino at Midnight), a fashion show of the 1988 Couture! collection, takes place at the Lope de Vega theatre in Madrid, ending with a grand finale of tricoloured flamenco clothing.

Moon Shadow S.r.l. becomes Moon Shadow S.p.A., a shareholding company.

Moschino clothes form part of the 'Fashion and Surrealism' exhibition at the Victoria and Albert Museum, London, organized by Richard Martin.

To Be or Not to Be: That's Fashion!, the catalogue of the 1988–89 Autumn/Winter collection, is published by Idea Books in Milan with photographs by Franco Moschino.

The 'XX Olimpiade della Moda' (Twentieth Fashion Olympics), the presentation of the 1989 Couture! collection at the Fiera di Milano, is interrupted mid-show by Franco

Moschino, who replaces it instead with the *Fashion Blitz* video explaining the dangers of fashion shows. It comes with the warning, 'Fashion shows can be dangerous to your health'.

1989

The first Moschino boutique opens at 12, Via Sant'Andrea, Milan, with a large rustic-style reception with fancy-dress parades of famous people (Roman centurions, harlequins, fairies, Queen Elizabeth, Olive Oil, Superman) and entertainment in the form of flamenco dancers, classical music and Neapolitan songs.

Nineteen paintings by Franco Moschino are displayed in the 'Collezione Vuoto' (Emptiness Collection) at the boutique in Via Sant'Andrea which is converted into a fake art gallery for the event.

Franco Moschino himself presents the press campaign for Spring/Summer 1989, dressing up as a different type of person for each collection to be publicized, wearing a blond wig to launch the Couture! line.

In November, a symbolic brick wall bearing pacifist messages and slogans is constructed in the window of the Via Sant'Andrea boutique to mark the collapse of the Berlin wall.

1990

'Stop the Fashion System' is the slogan that accompanies the advertising campaign based on a drawing of a vampire personifying Fashion. The same campaign becomes the subject of a ballet/fashion show at the Fiera di Milano in which the models, dressed as vampires, present Fashion being defeated by dancing gnomes.

In Madrid, Moschino is awarded the Aguja de Oro '90 (Golden Needle) award, the most prestigious Spanish fashion prize.

A boutique opens at 14, Via Durini, Milan.

1991

A large reception at Saks Fifth Avenue celebrates the launch of Moschino perfume in New York.

1992

The first press campaign that is markedly 'committed' is launched, dealing with issues such as drugs, animal abuse, and violence.

A charity fashion show in aid of the London Symphony Orchestra, 'The London Symphony Orchestra Moschino Fashion Event', is organized at the Grosvenor House Hotel in London to present the 1993 Couture! collection.

1993

A retrospective celebration of ten years in business entitled 'X Anni di Kaos! 1983–1993' (X Years of Kaos) features an exhibition at the Museo della Permanente in Milan, a book published by Lybra Imagine, a video distributed by RCS and a fashion show at the Teatro Nazionale in Milan.

For the tenth-anniversary 1994 Couture! collection some of the most successful and memorable garments are reproduced, under the 'Repetita Juvant' (Ever Appropriate) label.

'Progetto Smile!' is launched to raise funds to take HIV-positive children on holiday, financed initially by money raised from the 'X Anni di Kaos!' project.

1994

'Ecouture!' is launched; it is the first ecological collection (1994–95) designed in environmentally friendly materials and dyes, under the 'Nature Friendly Garment' label.

Moschino sponsors the exhibition 'Michelangelo, an Invitation to Casa Buonarroti' at the Accademia Italiana delle Arti in London, producing some specially hand-painted garments that are auctioned to raise money for the Accademia.

On 18 September Franco Moschino dies.

The Spanish foundation Amor a la Vida (Love for Life) awards Franco Moschino the Amor a los Animales (Love for Animals) prize, which is presented in Madrid to Signora Rossella Jardini by Her Majesty Queen Sofia of Spain.

1995

The slogan 'Moschino Forever' accompanies a display of various large-scale sculptures representing memorable Moschino 'symbols' (among them, a cow, a heart, a symbol of peace and Smile!) which are exhibited in a number of locations throughout the city of Milan.

In New York, the Michael Award is presented in memory of Franco Moschino.

In July the Franco Moschino Foundation is set up; it continues and expands the work of the Smile! project, providing support and help for HIV-positive children, in both Italy and Romania.

'Tribute to Moschino', a large concert featuring a range of musical genres, is organized, in collaboration with Pitti Immagine, to launch the menswear Spring/Summer 1996 collection at the Sferisterio delle Cascine in Florence. At this event, the mayor of Florence, Primicerio, awards the Premio Speciale Pitti Immagine to Franco Moschino.

1996

Two new perfumes, 'Cheap and Chic by Moschino' and 'Oh! de Moschino', are launched, and their publicity campaigns win important prizes.

At the first Florence Biennale, Moschino takes part in the 'New Persona, New Universe' exhibition, put together by Germano Celant at the Stazione Leopolda in Florence, by creating a huge heart-shaped maze installation.

To present the menswear Autumn/Winter 1996–97 collection, a theatrical performance entitled 'I Vestiti Nuovi del Re' (The Emperor's New Clothes) is organized. The show is loosely based on the fairy tale by Hans Christian Andersen with music by Gioacchino Rossino and is staged at the Manzoni theatre in Milan.

A number of new boutiques open: in Via Borgognona, Rome, on Rodeo Drive, Los Angeles, and on Madison Avenue, New York.

An auction, 'Art is Love', takes place in collaboration with Sotheby's at the opening of the New York boutique. Artists such as Julian Schnabel, George Condo, Donald Baechler, Arman and John Baldessari donate works to be sold. The profits are given to Hale House, an organization providing support for children of alcoholics and drug addicts in Harlem.

1997

New boutiques open in Osaka, Bangkok, and in Via Belsiana, Rome.

'Sarajevo 2000' is the campaign in which Moschino participates as a sponsor of the fundraising exhibition 'Artisti per Sarajevo' (Artists for Sarajevo) at the Querini Stampalia Foundation in Venice. Profits will be used to construct a contemporary art museum in Sarajevo.

The second men's aftershave 'Uomo?' is launched.